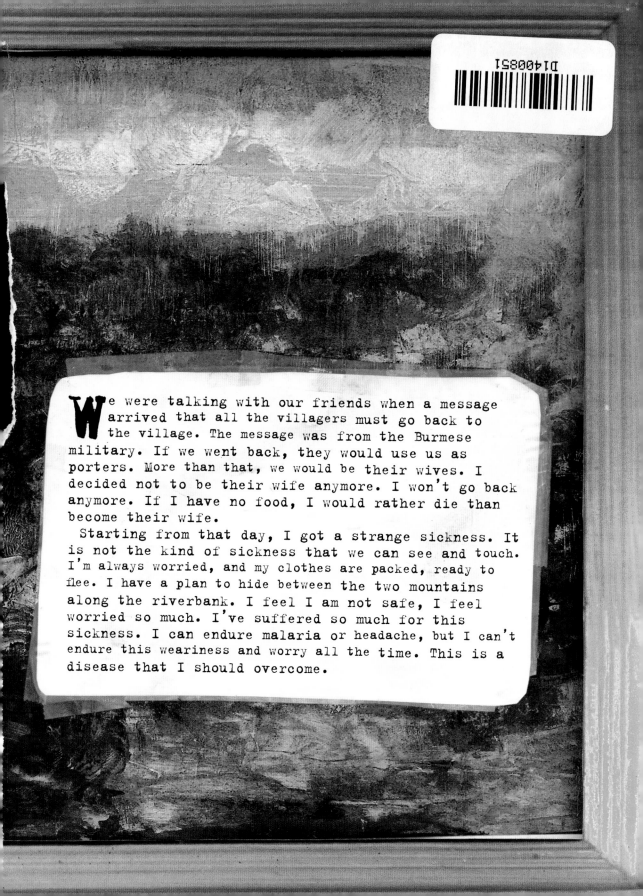

We were talking with our friends when a message arrived that all the villagers must go back to the village. The message was from the Burmese military. If we went back, they would use us as porters. More than that, we would be their wives. I decided not to be their wife anymore. I won't go back anymore. If I have no food, I would rather die than become their wife.

Starting from that day, I got a strange sickness. It is not the kind of sickness that we can see and touch. I'm always worried, and my clothes are packed, ready to flee. I have a plan to hide between the two mountains along the riverbank. I feel I am not safe, I feel worried so much. I've suffered so much for this sickness. I can endure malaria or headache, but I can't endure this weariness and worry all the time. This is a disease that I should overcome.

I can't sleep, I can't eat. I hear my heartbeat
all the time. I can't breathe, and I tremble.

I have no appetite.

I think nobody in the world can cure my disease.

At nine o'clock while we were worshipping in
church, we heard dogs barking, and the shooting.

"We know that your husband is not home. Be quick. We must leave
now. Which way to go, how many days it will last, we don't know."

The only way to flee was to climb a high mountain full of thorns and
bushes. No way for a human, but we must go to save our lives.

Who will cure me and make me healthy again?
Nobody in the world, unless God cures me.

A Karen boy drew this picture of a Burmese
army attack on his refugee camp.

I got bleeding for a day and a night. No strength to walk, and no medicine to use. I had an abortion and bled. That made me giddy.

I tried hard to overcome the difficulty.

We started our journey into Thailand.

It's a tedious journey for the small children.

It took ten days to reach the border.

Thai solders came to intimidate us. They came with a truck to send us back to Burma.

God did not allow them to do this.

CAMP UMPHANG

❧ DAY ONE, THAILAND-BURMA. LATE MORNING. ❧

The air hangs heavy, like a rubber tarp above my bobbing head.
Sitting atop oil drums and bags of rice, we fly through the
jungle in the back of a rusty blue truck.

   The road becomes steep as we travel higher and higher; we
pass through dense jungle and burning fields of rice. Green and
gray blur with the dust from the road. We stop often, picking
up women dressed in longyis. They, too, climb into the back.
Their faces are striped with sandalwood paste and they look only
at the road ahead.

We stop at military checkpoints where our driver, an illegal Karen with forged Thai papers, whispers things unknown to the police. Here, I learn to be invisible. By the time we get to the camp, we are covered in dust, rain, and sweat. I am like the jungle's shivering palm leaf.

The camp itself is isolated and peaceful. I'm taken to a hut where the camp elders greet me. Did I know that the Thai government does not allow them, the Karen, to leave the camp? Most have no papers, passports, or work visas. They have no access to television or news, certainly not to the Internet. Their food is given to them by human rights organizations or painstakingly grown within the barbed wire fence. Most often, it is collected illegally outside these boundaries.

The elders recount their stories listlessly, absently, like the safety procedures on an airplane. How they fled into nighttime jungles, hearing the fiery lisp of their villages burning in the hands of the Burmese Tatmadaw soldiers. How they ran and ran - babies, pots and pans, and food strapped to their backs, panting, terrified, sweating, falling again and again onto the wet earth. And they would pick themselves up and stumble onward into the unknown. They could only imagine the firestorms obliterating rice fields that had been in their families for generations. Their cherished pets being killed. They ran — men, women, and children hiding in the jungle trees like moths. They became part of the night, muzzling their babies at every sound, surviving on rice and bark. And if they did not escape, they became mute witnesses to rape or watched as their loved ones disappeared into forced labor.

As they speak, the deep lines on the elders' faces become indecipherable maps.

AN Abbreviated List of Everything That is Wrong with DON BAN YANG CAMP:

- Starvation.
- There is nothing to do.
- The bamboo huts are falling down on one another. It's as though a storm has imploded within these walls and the camp's inhabitants simply exist in its aftermath.
- Having to wait for food to be given them by N.G.Os.
- Why are they being held here like prisoners?
- Being forced to work outside the camp illegally.
- No one has money.
- Who do they tell when they are raped and abused? Who is protecting them?
- They need medicine.
- Some are forced to take yabba (like speed) in order to work without exhaustion.
- They have no legal rights.
- They need books and school supplies.

- The walkway of each "street" is maybe three meters long. The houses are inches apart. The ground is infused with shit, vomit, and piss from animals and people. Kids run around naked.
- Do their homes still exist?
- Abortion is performed by stabbing into the uterus with a stick or a cotton swab. The woman bleeds the baby out.
- There is no privacy.
- The stick can become lodged inside the uterus, causing heavy internal bleeding.
- They are starving for everything.
- Rape outside the camp is a common occurence.
- Of those who become pregnant, many are forced to abort.
- I can't find a bathroom.
- When can they go home?

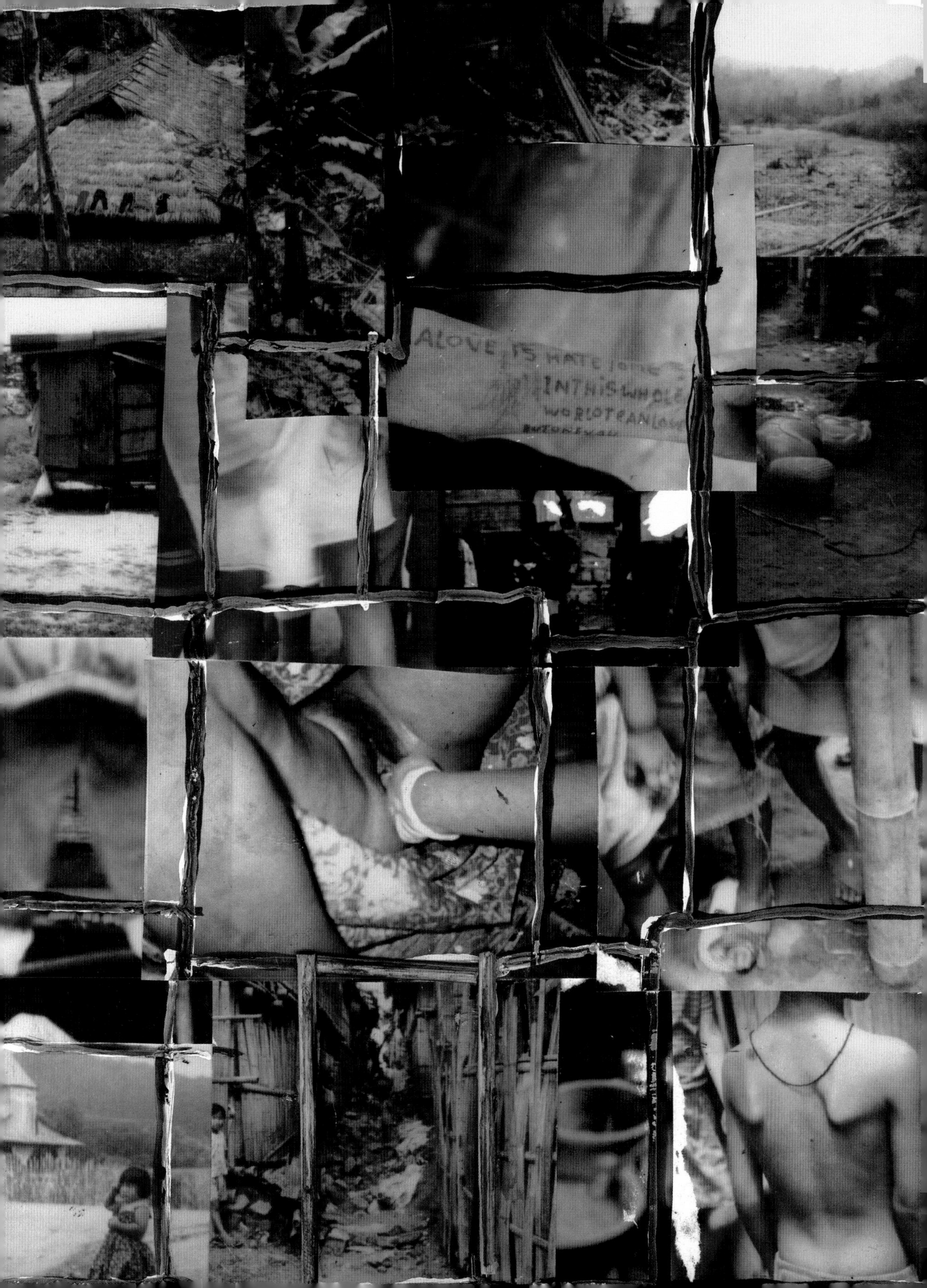
ALOVE IS HATE
INTHISWHOLE

This red string is for you, Mama.

The story of a girl's life in the camps, inspired by the people of Tham Hin and Don Ban Yang.

Dear Mama,

This is a kind of letter, though I am writing most of it
in my heart, for you, for me, for a time when I can speak
it. This torn and bloodied sheet should be enough, but words
bring clarity.

My first thought after it happened was that I should
wash the sheet. I should take it home and wash the shame
from it. But something stayed my hand. I was afraid to take
the sheet at first, afraid of him. For what seemed like a
long time, I couldn't look at him. But it couldn't have been
that long because his shadow on the floor didn't move. When
I looked, his eyes didn't meet mine. I guessed he was about
forty. Maybe it was his graying hair. There are many stories
in the camp about men like this, ordinary men who, because
we are at their mercy here in Thailand, take advantage of us
like this. A rage blacker than any mud came over me and I
grabbed the sheet. At first I meant to strangle him with it
but hesitated when I saw him stir; saw the hate in his eyes
return. Instead I swallowed the bitter taste in my mouth and
stuffed the sheet into the small raffia bag I had brought. You
must take me back to the camp now, I said. You must take me
home.

On the ride back, sitting shakily on the back of his
motorcycle, the wind was like ice on my skin. I knew it
wouldn't be long before the rain came. I had nothing to cover
myself with. The man was wearing a yellow rain slicker that
ensured he would stay warm and dry. I had no choice but to
wrap myself in the sheet, I thought. I pulled one end of the
bloodstained cloth out of my bag. It fluttered in the wind
like a sail. I couldn't use it as a wrap. It would have felt
more like a funeral shroud. I stared at it for a moment.
There were two loose threads tickling my wrist. When I got
home, I plucked them. One red string I tied around a flower
and hid in the bamboo rafters, the other I tied around my
wrist. This is the old way, Mama.

As we rode on that unstable motorcycle, I shoved the
cloth back into the raffia bag and wrapped my arms instead
around the body of the man who had raped me. For balance; for
safety. The first drop of cold wetness hit me and I thought,
let it rain, that is better than wrapping death around me.

It is still raining, Mama. The way it does here. One
drop first and then all at once. I used to play as a
child in the rain back home. There is something essential
about this rain. It feels right.

We are Christians now, but if I had money, I would set
a date for the great sacrifice and have the priest kill a boar
and a white chicken as I confess my sins to the Lords of Land
and Water. But I can tie my wrist. I still remember what you
taught me, even here, even here without you. This red string
is for you.

Dear Boy,

I don't know your name otherwise I would use it. So I call you boy, because that is what you are. I think of you as an angel because from the bottom of that ditch where we hid from your patrol, the sun was bright through the rain. And you, the youngest soldier, followed a few steps behind. You stopped when you saw me there alone. Framed against the fan of sunlight, you looked like an angel. I knew you could see me, I knew because your gun was pointed at me. That is why I am writing this unspoken letter in my heart and believe that you will hear me.

I have often wondered why you spared me. Was it to spare yourself the consequences of my death? Or was it because you looked into my eyes and saw something that kept you from pulling the trigger?

I feel pity for you, even though you soldiers have treated us like animals. I am Karen, my mother taught me to say even as a child. To say it like this - ko ren. Like the fish? I asked, and she said, and why not? Our ancestors crossed the Gobi, the river of running sand, to come to our homeland.

It was raining when the first soldiers came, raining and night darker than water in a well. At first we thought the mortars were thunder, the flash of tracer bullets like lightning. But it was soldiers like you, and soon everything was noise and fire and smoke. People running, screaming. That's when I lost my mother. I saw my father begging for our lives as we ran out the back of the hut and into the jungle. I saw as they cut him down like a weed. And then I ran into the rain and the dark wet steaming jungle and lost both of them.

In the morning, I walked out of the jungle into the burnt skeleton of my village. Most of the villagers were back and they had buried nearly all the dead. I walked to the edge of the hill, the one that falls down into the valley. From there I used to pretend I could see the whole world, and a river whose name I have forgotten. That morning, it was just a deep ravine with a river.

I couldn't find my parents or our house at first and probably never would have if I hadn't found our neighbor's son, twelve like me, sitting on the floor by the remains of

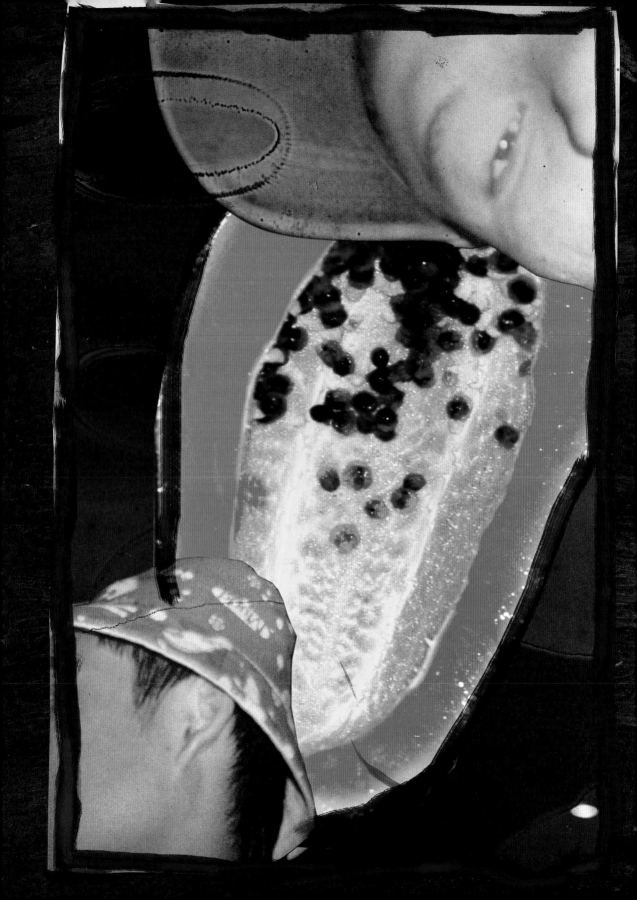

his home. Both his parents were dead, too, leaving him with his baby sister. I forgot myself at this sight. I tried to take the baby from him but he fought me, so all day I sat next to him as he pressed her to his chest, letting her suckle at his nipple. Together we stared into the distance. It was hours before I realized the baby had died. Later, before dark, the elders gathered the survivors and we all left for the safety of the jungle, sure the soldiers would return.

I cannot remember much about that time in the jungle hiding. Only little things, like a bird flashing by, red and rude against the jungle walls so green and dark they could have been the face of night. Staring with surprise at my reflection in a clear pool; eyes that held irises so black, a square face that made me look like a boy. My mother used to say I had a smile like a butterfly landing on her palm. One morning, a few days into the jungle, I woke to a woman wailing over her dead dog and it wasn't long before other mourners joined her. It is a sad sight: a rainy dark jungle and a woman crying over a dead dog. They weren't crying for her dog, though.

I remember pulling leeches from my skin with a joy that is hard to describe. When they popped off they left a bleeding wound, red against my dark olive skin, a wound that stung. It felt good, that stinging. We ate what we could find, worms, grubs, bananas and even insects, but no meat. It was always raining so hard we couldn't cook anything. We couldn't even make a fire to keep us dry, to keep warm by, and soon, our clothes began to rot on us. By the third week we had all lost our shame. We went to the toilet within eyesight of each other, men and women. It felt safer to be no farther than a quick glance from each other. My period came on that trek through the jungle. I had no rags to staunch it like I had seen my mother do, so I let it run down my leg. The rain took it all.

My mother used to say that rain here pours like a blessing, like a thick veil that parts to reveal the bride's face. But nearly every day, when this rain parted, it revealed a long line of soldiers, like you, like death, marching toward us, and we would scatter with a practiced silence and hide. Six weeks after we first went to hide in the jungle, we were found by a group of Karen guerrillas. They led us out of the jungle. Warned us about the paths and showed us how to avoid the mines. They led us to a refugee camp.

I feel bad because I pity you, boy, soldier, because it feels like a betrayal of my people, and of my dead parents. I wonder, boy, if you are still alive.

```
===============================
```

Sing with me.

Camp: rickety shelters we would never have
put our animals in, packed in tight rows like
the pretend houses children might build;
hunger; narrow streets running through this
shantytown, each a river of filth and shit even
the dogs avoid; hunger; scavenging the already
barren countryside by the river for food;
hunger; sickness, diarrhea; hunger; rain and
more rain; hunger. It is hard to hold on to all
that we were before we came here.

Sing with me. I was so young when you left
me, Mama, but I can remember the verse of
poetry you sang as you cooked, mixing your
grief in with the food:

God took the foam of water
It becomes banyan's flower
Foam of water god's taking
Keh taw weh ler kler ah klee
It becomes a banyan's seed

Sometimes I want to be the banyan seed,
to hold all of Buddha's enlightenment in my
heart. I heard about Jesus and the angels
in this camp, and sometimes I want to be an
angel. Between my house in this camp and the
one next to it is just enough space for me
to spread my arms. Every day I place my arms
against the wood beams of the two houses and
hold them there, pushing outward with
all my strength. When I step out and
hold my arms down, they rise into wings by
themselves and it feels like flying.

```
===============================
```

Dear Rapist,

I wasn't afraid when you came on your motorcycle to hire someone to clean your house. I wasn't afraid because I was hungry. I had heard stories of men like you, but I wasn't afraid because going anywhere, doing anything, seemed better than waiting for the slow death of starvation in the camp. And there was always the chance that you would be a good man; that you would have work and food for me.

I try to tell myself that it wasn't my fault. That if death comes to you wearing a safe face, it is hard to run. We rode for a long time until we came to a hut in the middle of some rice fields. You parked your motorcycle and pulled me off. I'm coming, I said, running to catch up. I had brought a small brush and rags in my raffia bag to clean with. It was a small hut and I would do a good job and be paid well. I would save to go back to school. Once inside the hut, you pushed me onto the small mattress with the dirty white sheet in the corner and tore my clothes. I didn't understand until I felt the pain.

I want to curse you. I want to curse you until your manhood shrivels up. I want to curse your unborn children and your wife and your mother and your father and your life. I want you to die. This is true. I want you to die.

It rained the whole ride back to the camp. I felt it on my head and I bent back and felt the cool water run off my face like tears. Did you know that I had enough rage to kill you even as I held on to you to keep from falling off your motorcycle? Did you feel the power of my eyes in your back? Perhaps not. Like my mother before me, I have learned to hide everything deep in my heart.

You dropped me off in the mud pit that is the entrance to the camp. Before you could roar off on your motorcycle, I reached out and scratched your face. A deep red line appeared. I did it to mark you, so that you would not forget me. You stopped, a shout on your lips, but you hesitated. I followed your gaze. By the river to the left I saw a line of women bent in the rain like a long sad caterpillar. I knew what they were doing. Searching for food, for some root they somehow missed the day before or the day before that. They rose as one, like a wave behind me, their eyes locked on you. You fled before all those ravenous eyes, ready to devour you.

I will be free of you.

I am free of you.

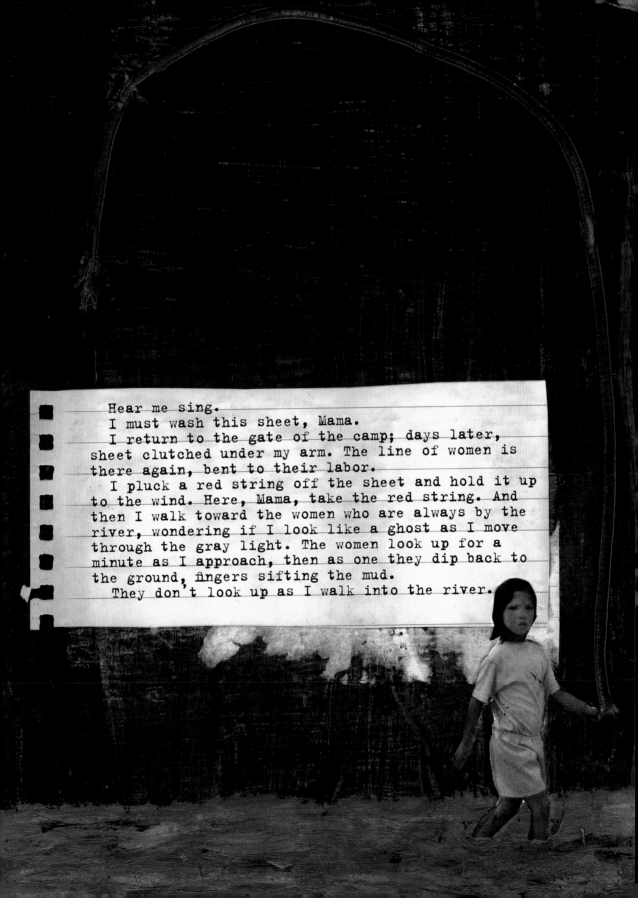

Hear me sing.
I must wash this sheet, Mama.
I return to the gate of the camp; days later, sheet clutched under my arm. The line of women is there again, bent to their labor.
I pluck a red string off the sheet and hold it up to the wind. Here, Mama, take the red string. And then I walk toward the women who are always by the river, wondering if I look like a ghost as I move through the gray light. The women look up for a minute as I approach, then as one they dip back to the ground, fingers sifting the mud.
They don't look up as I walk into the river.

Self portraits

She took one picture every hour

while working her shift at the brothe

She had 6 clients in 12 hours.

HOTEL ROOM MAE SOT
P.M.

Saw-Po, a Karen woman who works for a local human rights organization, makes me change my clothes and brush my hair. She even asks me to put on perfume. She's concerned that my crumpled T-shirt makes me look like a backpacker and we will not be allowed into the brothel that we are about to visit.

She likes to tell jokes that don't end and is prone to walking way too fast.

We arrive on the back of Saw-Po's moped; we had traveled a maze of narrow, damp streets, past vendors in outdoor markets selling fried cockroaches, mangoes, underwear, and pirated DVDs. Our arrival was a crashing decrescendo, the motor dying with a gasoline cough. I am now a student writing a paper on STDs, Saw-Po tells me. That will get me through the door.

The brothel is in a noodle shop. A few people slurp soups fragrant with chilies and mint. Some peel the skins of durian fruit, their hands wet with juice. There's an unmistakable scent of lemongrass and laundry detergent.

We walk through the restaurant into an outdoor atrium. There, girls sit on the cement washing clothes or brushing their long black hair. It's serene and social, the kind of scene that might be depicted in the pastel paintings that are sold on street corners all over Mae Sot.

We're shown into the room of one of the sex workers. Her door is one of many; the courtyard looks like a horse stable. Inside, her room is a shock of fuchsia and glitter and posters of Thai movie stars. Empty chip bags and makeup line the wooden walls. Lots of unfinished ideas in the chaotic piles of clothes and books. The door is locked behind us. It's hard not to feel vulnerable in a locked room. I have been told to be careful - a Western man was shot in this brothel last week.

I whisper as I talk to the girl in the glitter-happy room. Figures stop outside the door to listen. I can hear the sound of fucking. Men coming. Dressing. Then leaving. That sticky smell of sex begins to permeate my hair and clothes.

I'm talking to a woman whose face is an opaque glaze of white pearl powder that hides acne scars. Kohl lines have melted into the rims of her eyes, turning them dark and glassy. Matte chrysanthemum lipstick is delicately drawn across her small mouth. She points to two mats on either side of the room. This is where they bring their clients.

Love is peace. Love.
While we are in this
world, if we have love,
we will have peace—we
will have God. If there
is no love we will be in
trouble. God is love.

Do the women feel strange about having sex in front of one another? Do the clients?

No. We just look away.

Yesterday, Saw-Po told me that this woman is HIV+. I'm thinking of all the men who she sleeps with, men who in turn might pass the virus along to other sex workers, maybe to their wives and maybe to their babies.

A couple of days earlier, I was in a clinic on the Burmese border. I stood in a cement room that smelled like fermenting leaves and urine. This naked baby boy crawled up to me and tugged my shorts. I picked him up. He leaned his head against mine and scooped handfuls of my hair into his mouth. His brown love-me eyes. I closed mine, and there we were, the two of us, suspended in this large smile.

The pediatrician whispered that the baby has AIDS, drawing out the word like a knife cutting into cardboard. The baby's parents are dead, and he will not have any access to medicine. It's simply too expensive.

Now, in the brothel, I'm overcome by the same feeling: not sadness, exactly, but a smothering reality.

This woman needs to continue to work; if she works, she can eat well and maybe eventually buy medicine. She can't let anyone know that she has HIV. She would rather talk about her horoscope, where she bought her black sandals, and the day she crossed the bridge into Thailand. She can cover up all the rest with white foundation and red lipstick.

The brothels along the Thai-Burma border are filled with refugee girls.
Their HIV/AIDS rate is about 25%. The walls of this brothel in Ranong are
covered with years of makeup graffiti.

The Princess of the Sagawa Tea Shop

A story of the brothels.

I will have to tell her. But I wait as long as possible. We all get our monthlies around the same time and Kyi May lets me wash out her rags, so the queen doesn't suspect anything. This time I have made a plan. What kind of plan, am I out of my mind?

Maybe. But in a crazy place that is not such a bad thing.

Last night, Karim came. He is big and smelly and the other girls never want to go near him, because he's Indian, and a Muslim, though of course a Muslim will never visit a brothel. No one visits the brothels, not Buddhists, Christians, or Muslims, but smell the white stink in our little courtyard on a Friday night! The men of all religions piss semen.

Karim, Karim, you do not *really* stink. Just turmeric and hair oil. Also, he is very hairy, and the girls hate this. But they are young; the new one is just fifteen. Our old bitch queen will only be happy when she has twelve-year-olds in here, I'm sure of it. If she wasn't so lazy, she'd go up to Tachilek and buy some little virgins.

This is my third place in five years. But I remember the early time, crying every day. The new girl is shocked, just like I was, she thought she'd come over the border to work as a maid. I thought I was coming here to sew in a factory. She still trembles when the men go near her. It's true that she's not a virgin anymore, but she's still a child. *Dow-ka amiagee shee-deh*, my mother always used to say, and I say it all the time now, too: There is much suffering in this world. It's the one thing you can depend on. That's what the Buddha said, too, and he certainly knew what he was talking about.

She'll get tougher. The crying every day, and the trembling, that will pass. I try to be kind to the young one. Kyi May does not like her, though, because she gets so much business. All the men want to fuck the new girl, especially on the weekend, and the new girl just wants to sob in her mummy's arms. Friday to Sunday are hell because they all get drunk and take forever to finish their business, the bastards. I gave her some cream to put down there; she says she's all raw.

I ask Karim why he doesn't want to go with the new girl and he frowns and looks at me like there's something wrong with my head. "Because I come to see you," he says. "And I feel sorry for her. Do you think I'm deaf? I hear her crying in her room." Her spot is straight across the little courtyard, where we wash our clothes and eat and sit around during the day if there's nothing to do. Surrounding the courtyard are our rooms, little places just big enough for a bed,

Condom
packagE

a low table, and then our clothes under the bed or on a shelf we make with old scraps. The walls are very thin, the rooms are dark. But the courtyard is open to the sky. We spend a lot of time out there, looking up.

Why wouldn't I take him, I always take this Indian, smelly and hairy, I don't care. He says he feels sorry for a crying little girl. Now that is a man! And he really doesn't go with her, I've checked. Karim, Karim, I will sleep the whole night with you whenever you can pay. We never take men for the whole night unless the man pays a lot, four or five times the normal amount of just one shot. No matter what we make, the queen takes more than half of it, for our room and board—and she takes almost everything from the new girls for more than a whole year, because they need to pay off their travel costs from Burma, and she has to pay the agent who brought them here. That's how it works! They sell us like animals and then we spend a couple of years paying them for selling us like animals. What kind of a world is this? *Dow-ka amiagee shee-deh.*

But the old bitch queen is just a mama-san, not a general. She's acts more like a military intelligence agent, but we all hate her so much that we don't spy on one another for her. Even if she hovers like a ghost at our plywood doors, listening, she cannot listen all the time. When Karim stays the whole night, there is time to talk. Time for whispering after sex like real lovers. Time to give me more money than usual. Karim. His name is like a pillow. If I'm scared she's at my door, he gets up to take a piss in the toilet between the rooms and the tea shop, and he checks around. Sometimes she's there, in the courtyard, floating around with her powdered face and red mouth, but when she sees him she runs away, out to the front. She's scared of him, because he's tall and black and isn't ashamed of anything.

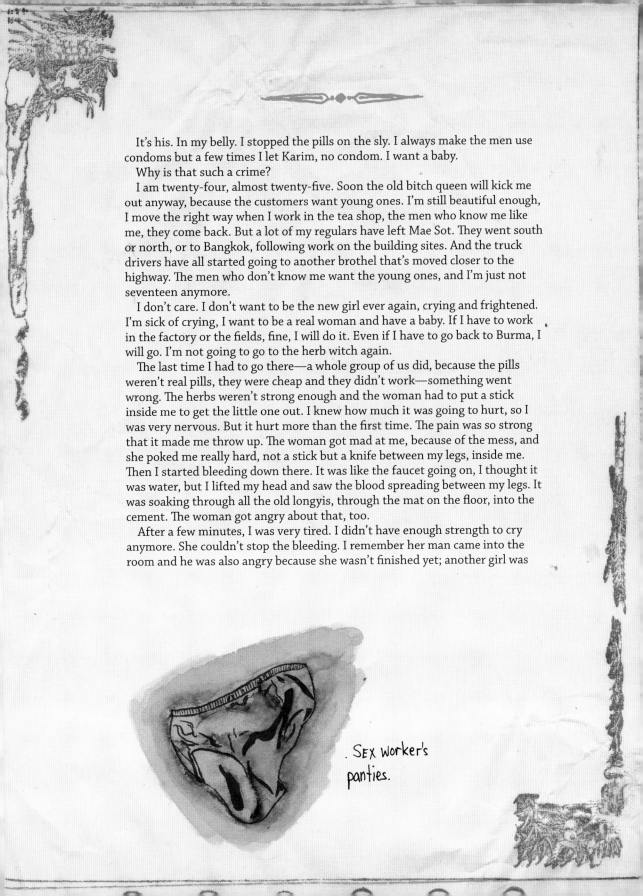

It's his. In my belly. I stopped the pills on the sly. I always make the men use condoms but a few times I let Karim, no condom. I want a baby.

Why is that such a crime?

I am twenty-four, almost twenty-five. Soon the old bitch queen will kick me out anyway, because the customers want young ones. I'm still beautiful enough, I move the right way when I work in the tea shop, the men who know me like me, they come back. But a lot of my regulars have left Mae Sot. They went south or north, or to Bangkok, following work on the building sites. And the truck drivers have all started going to another brothel that's moved closer to the highway. The men who don't know me want the young ones, and I'm just not seventeen anymore.

I don't care. I don't want to be the new girl ever again, crying and frightened. I'm sick of crying, I want to be a real woman and have a baby. If I have to work in the factory or the fields, fine, I will do it. Even if I have to go back to Burma, I will go. I'm not going to go to the herb witch again.

The last time I had to go there—a whole group of us did, because the pills weren't real pills, they were cheap and they didn't work—something went wrong. The herbs weren't strong enough and the woman had to put a stick inside me to get the little one out. I knew how much it was going to hurt, so I was very nervous. But it hurt more than the first time. The pain was so strong that it made me throw up. The woman got mad at me, because of the mess, and she poked me really hard, not a stick but a knife between my legs, inside me. Then I started bleeding down there. It was like the faucet going on, I thought it was water, but I lifted my head and saw the blood spreading between my legs. It was soaking through all the old longyis, through the mat on the floor, into the cement. The woman got angry about that, too.

After a few minutes, I was very tired. I didn't have enough strength to cry anymore. She couldn't stop the bleeding. I remember her man came into the room and he was also angry because she wasn't finished yet; another girl was

. Sex worker's panties.

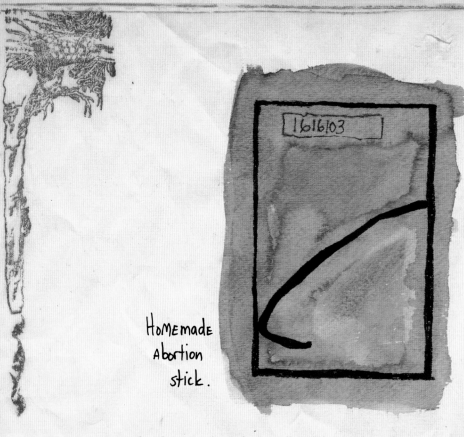

HoMEMade
Abortion
stick.

1616/03

waiting. When he came closer, he saw all the blood. He was frightened. His big
eyes showed his fear, but I didn't care, I was falling asleep. The weight of the
pain pulled me down. It was easier to close my eyes and sink with it.

Going to sleep, I thought, I need to say good-bye in my mind to Mother
and Father, because I will never see or speak to them again. I remembered the
river near the village where I was born, how I played in the water when I was a
child. I used to hold my breath and sink to the bottom, to touch the silt, and all
the sounds were muted. Like this. You knew there was noise up above, on the
surface—especially when men came after work to wash their elephants—but
none of the voices could touch you. I thought how I loved everything, my
parents, my brothers and sisters who used to swim with me, even the elephants
and the river, and the narrow path through the trees that led up the hill to our
house. But I would never go home now.

I said good-bye in my heart to Ameh and Apeh. I thanked them for my life,
such as it was. Then I thought, Now I will die.

Sometimes you wonder why you don't die.

What is the purpose of staying alive if it is only this, the Sagawa Tea Shop.
My family so far away. No little children. Sagawa flowers are the flowers for
weddings and love, but I have never seen even a dead sagawa blossom in this
dirty place.

The abortionist's man took me to Dr. Cynthia's clinic. He was truly afraid.
What would they do with my dead body and just a room full of blood? Then my
mama-san wouldn't even pay them for the abortion.

The people at the clinic saved my life. My own crying woke me up, because the medicine they gave me for the pain had worn off. While I was sleeping, they put new blood in me and took out the stick, which had made a hole in my womb, and they took out the little one, too. The doctor came and said, "If you ever have an abortion again, it will kill you. Your womb won't heal easily; the damage is very bad. We had to give you a lot of blood to keep you alive. And nothing was clean at that woman's house, so your blood has been poisoned."

And she told me I'd probably never be able to have a baby anyway.

Three days later I was back at work.

But I *am* going to have a baby. This baby.

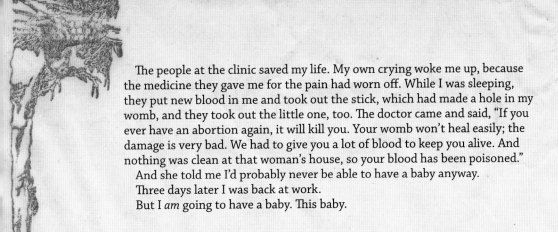

Last night Karim comes to visit me and we lie in the dark, whispering. I tell him I want to leave the Sagawa. I've made a plan and asked around at the market. I lie and tell him I've saved enough money for one month's rent and some food. Really I have enough for two months' rent. It will be a very small room in a house with others, the kitchen and the latrine outside shared. I will do another job. The factory, the building site, the fields, someone will hire me.

I tell him I'm getting too old. The mama-san and her husband are going to kick me out. I don't tell him about the baby. He will say it isn't his. What man wants a *pha tha ma* to have his child? No man born on this earth, even a good man.

I am lying in his arms and he is looking down that long nose at me. I ask him to help me. Not forever. Just the same way he helps me now. To visit like this sometimes, once or twice a week, to pay. After I've moved. Even though I don't mention the baby, he still looks at me like I'm trying to cheat him. I feel my neck under my hair get very hot. "Why are you looking at me like that?"

He keeps staring. His bushy eyebrows meet over his nose and his eyes are squeezed together, so his thick eyelashes look like caterpillars. "Because there is something else."

"What?"

"Something you are not telling me."

But I make some noise, and kiss him, and get on top of him and swing my hair over his face. I do not tell. If I tell, he will not help me. Instead we have more sex and I keep my secret. He agrees to help me, to still visit me when I leave. He talks like a lover, very romantic. I often wonder if he ever talks to his wife this way. The talk is sweet but not useful. I also feel love for him, but I am not a young girl anymore, I make those feelings small. They're like the little candles we used to put up on the walls around the temple compound during festival nights. They were so pretty, and extravagant, yellow glittering along the walls. But in the morning, everything's just the way it always was. The candles are gone, all the wax is melted into the brick. When night comes again, it's dark as usual.

The next day—I stop washing my clothes in the courtyard—I stand up and tell her, "Three months, it's not coming."

She screams. Puts her head back and howls with a twisted-up face, a monkey with its hand in a beehive. I stand in front of her in my blue tamin, the prettiest one. I am sucking in my stomach. It's not three months. It's four.

"Didn't you take your pills, one pill every day? They were good pills, not fakes. Dumb girl!" She bends over, takes off her slipper, and starts to hit me. Not in the face, but very hard, on the thighs, and then up higher, on my stomach. Whap whap whap. I don't move. Why bother? She's getting fat and she's not so strong. It's her husband I'll have to watch out for, he would be happy to punch me in the face. But she's lazy. She's just a barren old cow.

It's true. There are no children in the tea shop. That's why she enjoys it, she likes it when we have to go to the herb woman. She yells, "You're going again!" Whap. "I'm sending you again, you bitch, you're not getting a spot of money for ten days. The third job! Maybe this time she'll kill you and I'll be free of you forever, you Burmese slut."

I don't know why she calls me a Burmese slut. She's half-Burmese, too, but it's her Thai half that hates us all. Half-Burmese, half-Thai, 100 percent bitch queen of the Sagawa Tea Shop just four streets over from the Burmese section of the Mae Sot market. She used to do the same work as us until she married the brothel-owner.

She is still screaming and slapping me with her slipper. I cry very loudly and put my hands over my face. I make as much noise as I can, howling, begging her to stop. If I don't get a job hauling wet cement, I will go to Rangoon and become an actress.

Kyi May sticks her head out of her room, and so does the new girl and Aye Pwint and fat Thee from Moulmein runs out of the bathing room with the soap still in her hair. The courtyard is suddenly full of girls flapping around like chickens, afraid to come too close, squawking, "What's happening, what's happening? What did Princess do?" That's a stupid nickname, I know, but the men always liked it.

She stops hitting me for a moment and swings her arms around like a crazy woman and screams, "All of you, go back to your rooms. Right now! You, too! Wait until U Win Oo comes back tonight, I'll make him beat that baby out of you." She hits me again, as hard as possible, across the face, but my hands are still there, so the sharp plastic edge hits my fingers. I let out a genuine scream and run off, crying.

Suddenly my tears are real, but I don't throw myself down on the bed and bawl my eyes out. There's no time, I have to get ready. For once in my life, it's a lucky thing I own so little. Packing my things won't take very long.

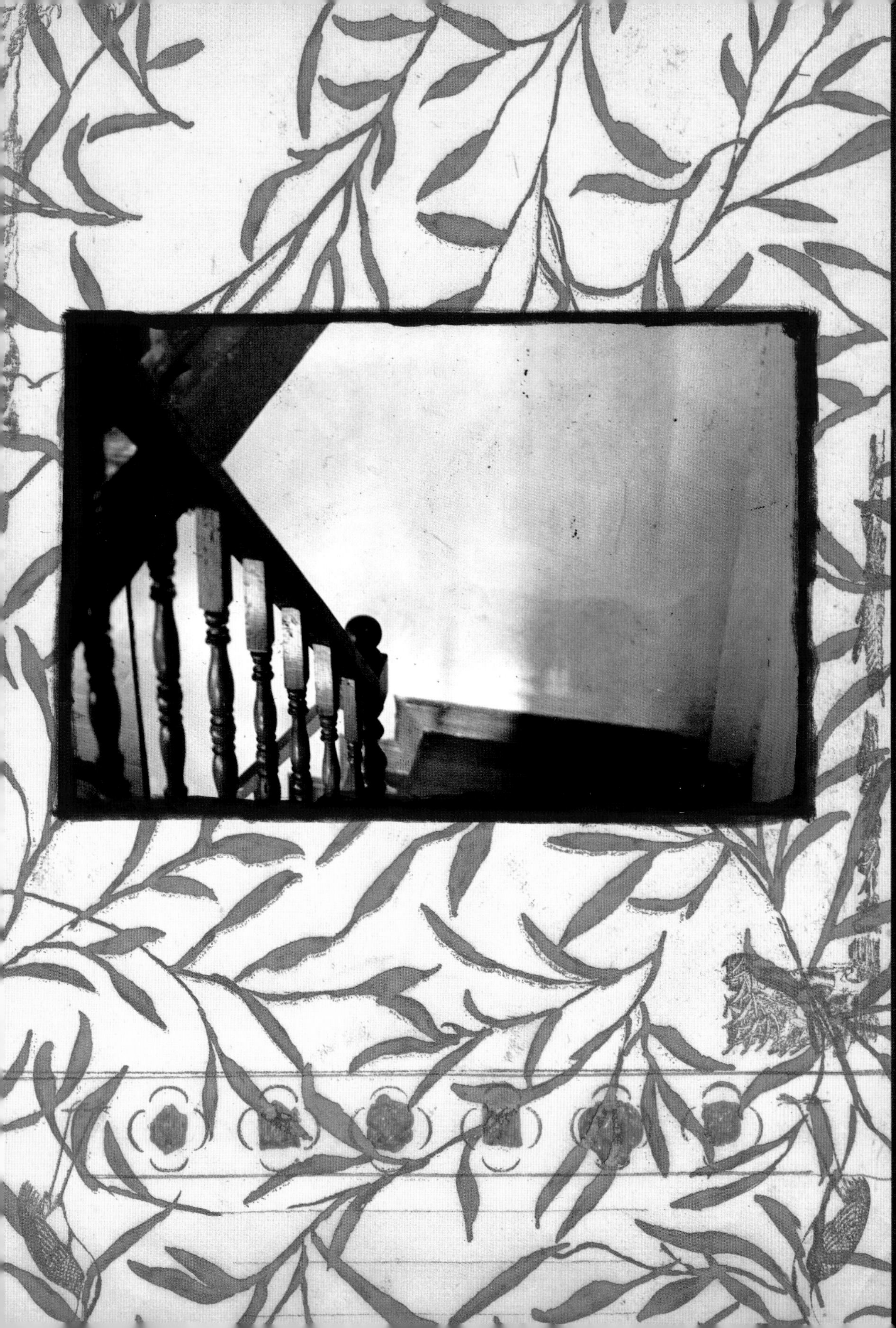

One Hour Away from Mae Sot

An hour earlier, it had started to rain. Little pellets that looked like dew. They made our skin silver as we walked to the boat that would take us back to Mae Sot. We stepped carefully, so softly, over thorny plants. The dust had turned to mud, splattering our shoes, socks, and legs. By the time we reached the boat, our clothes were clinging to our flesh and stained with the bloody remains of mosquitoes.

Bursts of gold on lavender melting into saffron. It's the time of day when the sky looks like it has been spray-painted by a graffiti artist. We cross the river and climb into our driver's car. I pull my bag close, feel the weight of the Polaroids, the writing from women and children.

We had been there illegally, the only way to see the tiny speck of land occupied by the Karen. Normally, when you enter Burma, you need a visa. You're only allowed to see villages and sights approved by the government.

Up ahead on the road, the Thai military signals us to pull over. The soldiers ask us to step out with our hands up. It's hot - the kind of heat that reduces everything to numbness.

Our driver hands the soldier his identification papers and work permit, all of the documents fake. The soldiers are pointing at me. I have no idea what anyone is saying, except that my guide, Victor, keeps bowing to tabletop perfection and is smiling a lot. I push my bra strap underneath my blouse and roll down my shorts. Some dirt falls out of the cuffs. I feel like a stupid amateur.

Tiny bubbles of spit have formed at the corners of our driver's mouth; like the rest of us, he has sweat stains under his arms. The tallest soldier takes my bag and dumps out the contents. The Polaroids, the dirt, my cameras.

The soldier looks at me as though I'm lying even though I haven't said a word. He hands me back the pictures with a nod. We can go.

As we drive away, I ask Victor to please explain.

"They pulled us over because they believed that we had entered Burma illegally and were doing research on child soldiers. They ask, 'Is this true?'"

His reply: "No. This girl is a Christian missionary, convincing Thai youngsters to embrace the faith and find salvation through Jesus."

In my mind I have a dream at the end of which I am living quietly and peacefully with my parents and my brothers again.

1 Cor · 13:13.

Prov · 3:5-6.

A bridge between Thailand and Burma.

"JOIN THE ARMY... OR GO TO JAIL!"

I met four Burmese soldiers ranging in age from 9 to 14. They had escaped from the Burmese army, and then were captured by the very people they were trained to kill: the Karen. I talked to them in a safe house on the border. These are their words.

Q. So continue. You were arrested. Why?
A. I was going to join the military or go to jail.
Q. Who came up to you?
A. The military.
Q. But who? Were they wearing uniforms?
A. Yes.
Q. And what did they do when they came up to you? Did they grab you?
A. They held my hands.
Q. And what did you say when they said you will be arrested or you join the military?
A. Yes, I said. I'll go to join the military.

My best friend is Yan. He was still at school and taking tuition classes in the evenings, and just like me he was picked up and taken off in a car one night. We were collected together and went together to the army classes. We finished the classes together and were both sent to the same brigade. We always thought the same. Like brothers, we two friends are really, really close.

HE WILL NEVER SEE THIS PLACE AGAIN...

The man in charge of the safe house asked me to keep the boys' identities a secret. If they return to Burma, they risk arrest for desertion.

One night I went about three hundred feet from my house to watch a film by the roadside. A Burmese love story. I was sitting on the side of the road. A car stopped. Two old men and four boys sat in the car. One of the men got out and grabbed me by the neck. And then I was handcuffed. They carried me. In the car, no one spoke.

The arrest took place between 8:00 p.m. and 1:00 a.m. I can't say when, exactly.

The car stopped and one big man started asking me questions. I knew not to ask anything myself. In my mind, I was thinking that I would never see my family again. I knew that I was being taken away to be a soldier. "If you try to escape, we will kill you," they said. "If you do escape, we'll kill your family."

The car went along the bus route to Rangoon. I could see houses, roads, trees. All I could think is that I would like one day to see my parents again. Some of the other boys in the car were crying. They were ten or twelve years old. They kept talking, asking why they were in the car, where they were going. The oldest man in the car asked each of them where they came from.

By the end of the night there were six boys in the car.

There are approximately 380,000 soldiers within the Burmese army — 1 in 5 is under 16 years of age.

I'M NOT AFRAID OF ANYTHING

Q. Are you afraid of anything?
A. Nothing.
Q. What about death?
A. No.
Q. No?
A. I'm not afraid of anything.
Q. Last time we met you said, "I'm not afraid of anything,
   I don't feel anything, I don't have any dreams, I don't
   want anything."
A. I'm not just pretending.
Q. I'm just trying to make sure it's true, what you said.
A. (translator) He is saying that because he believes. He
   really believes this. He believes in his statements.

Q. "I am not afraid of anything. I do not feel anything. I
   do not want anything."
A. (translator) He believes in what he is saying.

HMAWBI HILL!!!

Hmawbi Hill. On the right side, there is a training center. There is also a big hall where all of the recruits stay. There were two hundred fifty boys there. The eldest was nineteen.

We attended four and a half months of training. Our guns, the M1, M2, G4, M4. We were each given ninety-two bullets. Five bullets a day. We also learned how to place and disassemble mines.

My gun was too heavy for me. When I fired the gun, I fell down. We had a bull's-eye target. If we shot the target four times, we would be given five hundred kyats. Some tried to run away. If they were caught, they were beaten and put into interrogation.

I was beaten when I did not hit the target. I tried my best but I could never hit the bull's eye.

This is what I was told: "You are trained to serve your country. The enemies are terrorists. The terrorists are Karen. This is Burma. Burma is for the Burmans. The Karen are trying to take the country. The Burmans are shorter. The Karen are tall. The Burmans are darker; the Karen, lighter."

The truck that kidnapped one boy for army duty. He couldn't read or write and shook when he told his story.

When we young soldiers reached the front, we two friends were
given orders to be messengers carrying information and orders
along the line. We took a car from the brigade headquarters.
At about 9:00 p.m. that night, we arrived at the Eighty-first
Brigade. At sunrise, we started our journey again and drove
all day until we arrived at the 355th Brigade. They gave us
rice and curry and then we slept until six in the morning, when
we resumed our journey, arriving at Myawaddy at 8:00 a.m. the
following day. From Myawaddy we had to march to Kyonewa village
and when we got there we were really tired. We had some food,
and straightaway had to start the journey again. We reached the
top of a mountain, slept on the mountain, and got up before
sunrise to meet up with a car. After driving all morning we
arrived at Warley. We stayed one night at Warley and then, at
7:00 a.m., drove up a mountain for a night at Kanehlay camp. The
next morning at sunrise, we packed our kit and marched on foot
up Bayinnaung Mountain. We reached the Bayinnaung camp by about
10:00 a.m., and then we were each given a sack of rice to carry
up to the front.

   When we got to the top of the mountain with the sack of rice,
we were really tired, but had to go back down again before we
got any food for the day. Even then, the captains got as much
as they liked and we had to cook our own food. Every day it was
frightening. The mountain was very steep and we had to carry
the heavy rice sacks, and even when we couldn't manage to carry
them, we just had to.

   In this way we lived on Bayinnaung Mountain, every morning
carrying sacks of rice or oil up the mountain to the front, then
coming back down, going back up the mountain with rice, and
coming back down. The captains had only their guns to carry,
and they would swear at us, hit us when we got tired. If we said
our backs hurt, or our skin was broken, they swore at us. After
about seven days I said I had a fever and couldn't carry the
rice that day. They swore at me.

   "You can't carry the rice? You have to!" And I had to carry
the rice.

FROM HERE WE
PORTERED RICE & CEREALS. (14, 15, 16 YRS. OLD)
THE PORTERS ARE ALSO ~~PRISONERS~~ + PRISIONERS
PRISIONERS.

KANEHLAY - BAYINAUNG?
ROAD.

STREAM

REST.
10 DAYS
SOME G
EXHAUST

A. 2003, February
18. From here, the
terrorists tried to
attack us, shoot us.
Q. The terrorists?
A. The terrorists. From
here, the terrorists
shot at us.
Q. Did you shoot back?
A. We used 81s, big, big
guns. Point-fives.
Q. 81s? Point-fives?
A. Salgads. It's the
same kind of gun.
Q. What did you use?
A. I couldn't carry
these because they're
very heavy, these guns.
Q. Salgads?

"THE TERRORISTS
SHOT AT US!"

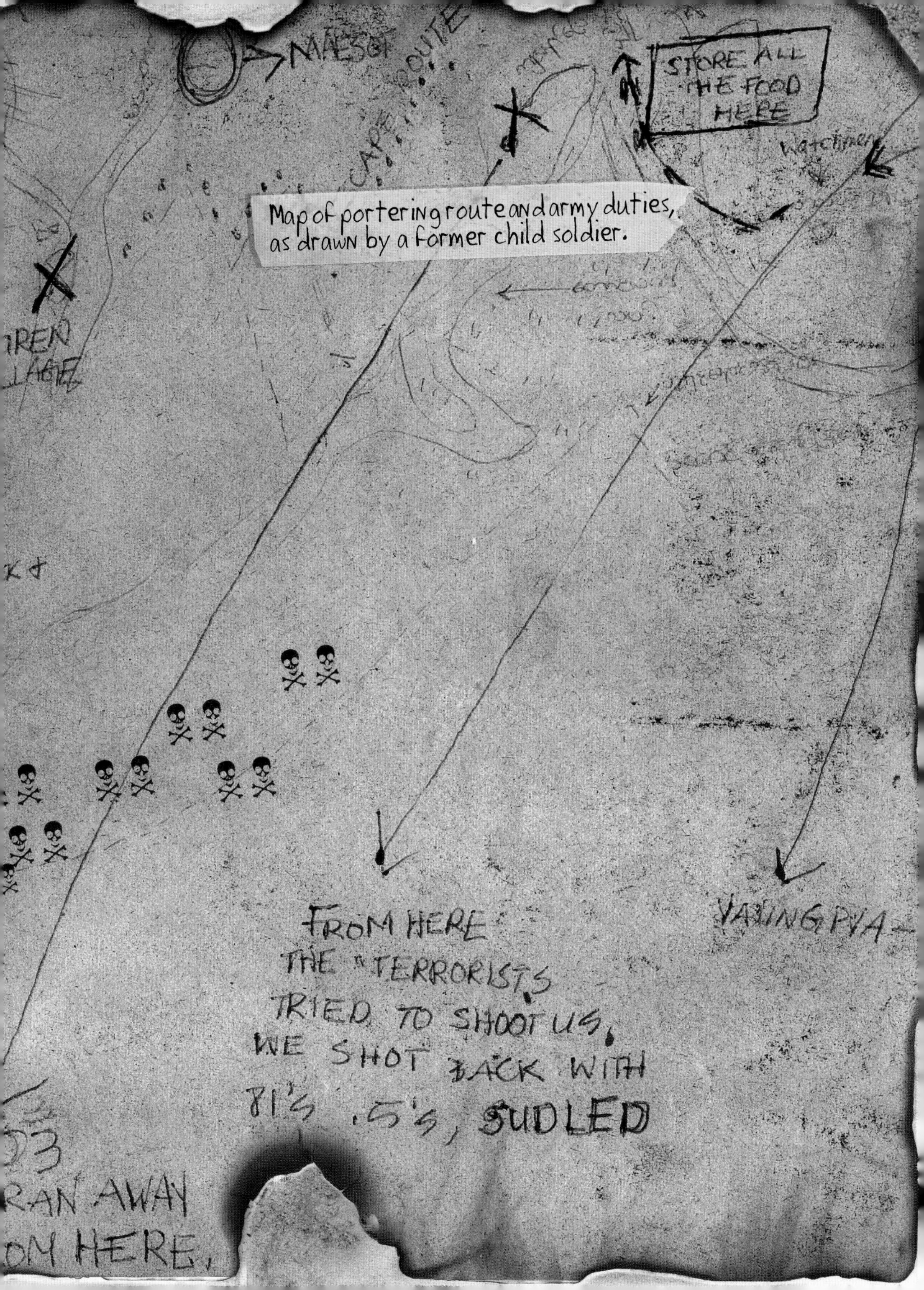
MAESOT
ESCAPE ROUTE
STORE ALL THE FOOD HERE
Watchmen
FROM HERE THE "TERRORISTS TRIED TO SHOOT US, WE SHOT BACK WITH 81'S .5'S, SUDLED
RAN AWAY
OM HERE.

Map of portering route and army duties, as drawn by a former child soldier.

There is this Karen mother in a poem. She has survived World War II, and continues to struggle in the hope of a chance to live life to the fullest in peace. Unfortunately, she finds herself again in another war—her country's civil war—and becomes a refugee in Thailand. She is a widow, a blind woman, and the mother of two sons. She lets her sons join the Karen National Liberation Army, hoping one day they will come home with victory.

During the famous Mae Tha Waw operation, she receives the news of one of her boys' death. She feels her mountain has fallen. As a blind person, it is the first time that she feels she understands the light. Her always-dark world has blackened. Still, she continues to endure. She walks to church every Sunday, a stick in her hand.

This woman's fate is long and ugly. It is in 1989 when the Burmese regime holds yet another major operation. The mother receives the news about her second son. This time she is brought to the body. Surrounded by the Karen soldiers, the mother begins to feel the body from the forehead to the toe, and from her blind eyes come tears. Very quietly this mother sobs, and it breaks all the men around her, and they cry.

DID YOU LIKE USING A GUN?

Q. Did you like using a gun?
A. Yes.
Q. Was it fun?
A. Yes.
Q. Why was it fun? Did you make friends?
A. Yeah.
Q. And you would talk to the other boys at night?
A. Yeah.
Q. What did you guys talk about?
A. We each said that we would run away.

In the morning Yan got his rice sacks, but I was left at the camp to help cook the rice and curry. I went down the hill to get cooking water, and on the way back up I met my friend coming back down the hill. The captains were doing nothing, just sitting around smoking, trying to blow smoke rings. Even though we had done nothing wrong, when they saw us, they hit us.

That day we both ate all the rice we could manage and at midday we ran away from Bayinnaung army camp as fast as we could. We crossed over two mountains, the rain started pouring down, but still we didn't stop. It was still raining as we two friends went to sleep in the jungle. Early in the morning we started up again. We decided that, even if we might step on a mine, like two brothers we would keep going. Then we got to the top of one hill and heard the noise of a car engine and a motorbike, so we continued that way, following a small stream until it got a bit bigger. We saw a man washing himself in the river, and we were happy.

An old Shan woman showed us how to get to the village, and we went through the village and ended up on a big highway that went to Bangkok, and on that road we met two men and asked them the way to Myawaddy. It was a long way, they said, why don't you come along with us and work for us, and we'll make sure nothing bad happens. So we went along with them. We followed along, and they gave us some food, and then they introduced us to their commander in the Karen National Liberation Army.

May I have a kiss from mommy. May I have a kiss from daddy. Not only from mom and daddy. A big kiss from teacher too.

And the head of the brigade said, "Why did you two run away? Where did you leave your guns?"

And we said, "Yes, we have run away, we have deserted from the Burmese army, because we had to carry rice sacks all day, we were beaten, and we couldn't stand it anymore."

And then they asked us more questions and put us in jail. We became very frightened because we saw four Burmese who had been captured by the Karen and accused of rape. One of the Burmese was killed several feet away from us with some kind of a knife, and we thought we were next.

But they looked after us well. Now we are fifteen years old. My friend was sent straight away to the Mae Sot 201st Battalion. We want to fight back. The Burmese army abused us. We would kill our abusers with a knife or a gun. We cannot forgive them.

If we do not die, we would like to meet our parents again.

Q. . . . .
A. So you could say I have never had an ordinary life.

A child soldier and his captain in the Burmese army.

 Mae Sot. Thailand.
Hotel room. Night.

The bathroom light is on, MTV Asia on mute.
Memory has caught me by the throat.
 I am walking along Patpong Road. It is a
sepia flurry of sound and image. The American
tourists are wide-eyed and slurring, hiding
their traveler's checks in defiant fanny
packs. I see them taking digital pictures
of young girls standing outside karaoke
 booths, flirty, their wanting breasts
   on offer.

        Patpong Road. The famous street in Bangkok
     where friends of mine once saw a girl shoot Ping-
   Pong balls out of her vagina. "One after the other," they
   told me. "Can you believe that vaginas can do that?"
   Now I know where those girls come from.
   I can't help but recall my own first encounters with a
 sexual underworld. The illicit thrill of going to the sex
 shows and the strip clubs. Sitting in the porn arcade
   giving a hand-job to the guy who sat in the back of
      my Russian Lit class.

Open-mouthed women on smudged screens sucking multiple dicks, the sounds of men jerking off in their own private booths - at the time, all of this was liberating. A big fuck-you to being a nice girl. We would leave these places and walk along Boulevard St.-Laurent, snow and ice making red tic-tac-toe patterns on our faces. It was a speedy feeling, as though we had crossed into another, more secret world.

I would go back to my dorm room alone. The familiar odors of condensed milk, pizza, du Maurier Lights, and pot, while the sounds of Portishead and Nirvana lulled me to sleep. At the time, it didn't even occur to me to wonder about the women in the porn videos. Why were they there? Where did they come from? Did they come from a family like mine?

Flickers of shadow and light on the ceiling of my darkened hotel room.

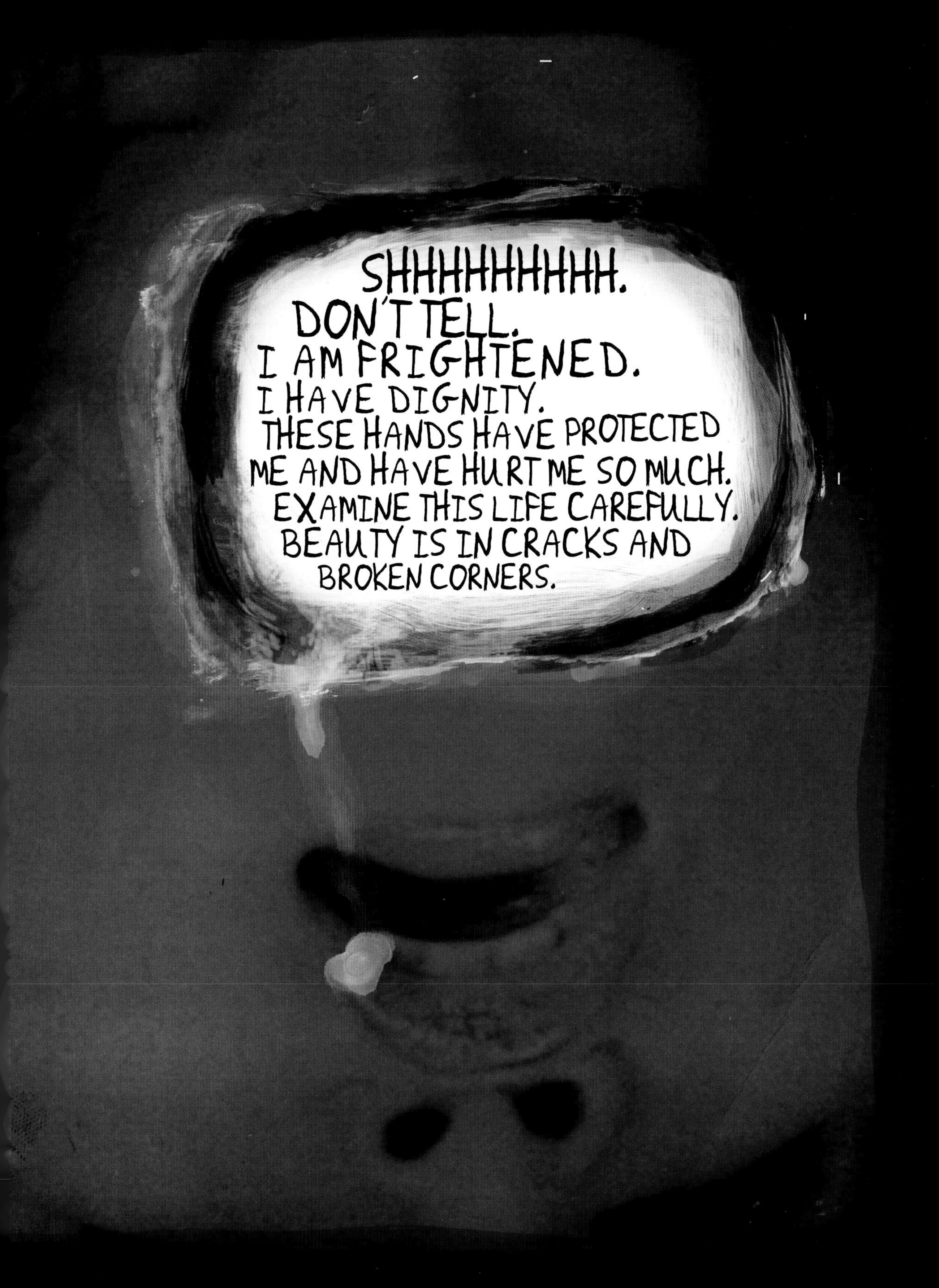
SHHHHHHHHH.
DON'T TELL.
I AM FRIGHTENED.
I HAVE DIGNITY.
THESE HANDS HAVE PROTECTED
ME AND HAVE HURT ME SO MUCH.
EXAMINE THIS LIFE CAREFULLY.
BEAUTY IS IN CRACKS AND
BROKEN CORNERS.

We are sitting against the wall of the brothel, she and I. It's late afternoon and we're whispering - she can barely speak.

She is 17 and terrified. She wants me to know that she has just started working in the brothel and that she is a very good student in school. She is planning to quit and cross the bridge back into Burma.

Her eyes.

I recognize those eyes. Eyelashes that protect you from seeing too much, and keep others from doing the same.

I was 17 when the man handed me the joint and said, "Like this, watch me. Inhale. Hold it in your lungs. Now breathe out. Close your eyes." It is laced pot. And then the floor is melting and sliding into the speaker. We are dancing in an after-hours club in someone's row house, and then we are in an apartment. His apartment. His face. Water that tastes like mercury sliding down my throat. His fists, tight, grabbing my hair, pushing me down, down, down.

My mother was waiting for me the next morning, her hair like a wayward hedge. She made me look in the mirror. My shirt was turned inside out. White crust on my face, the fly of my leatherette pants ripped.

There is nothing unusual about my story. But it was the last time, until now, that I examined these things so closely.

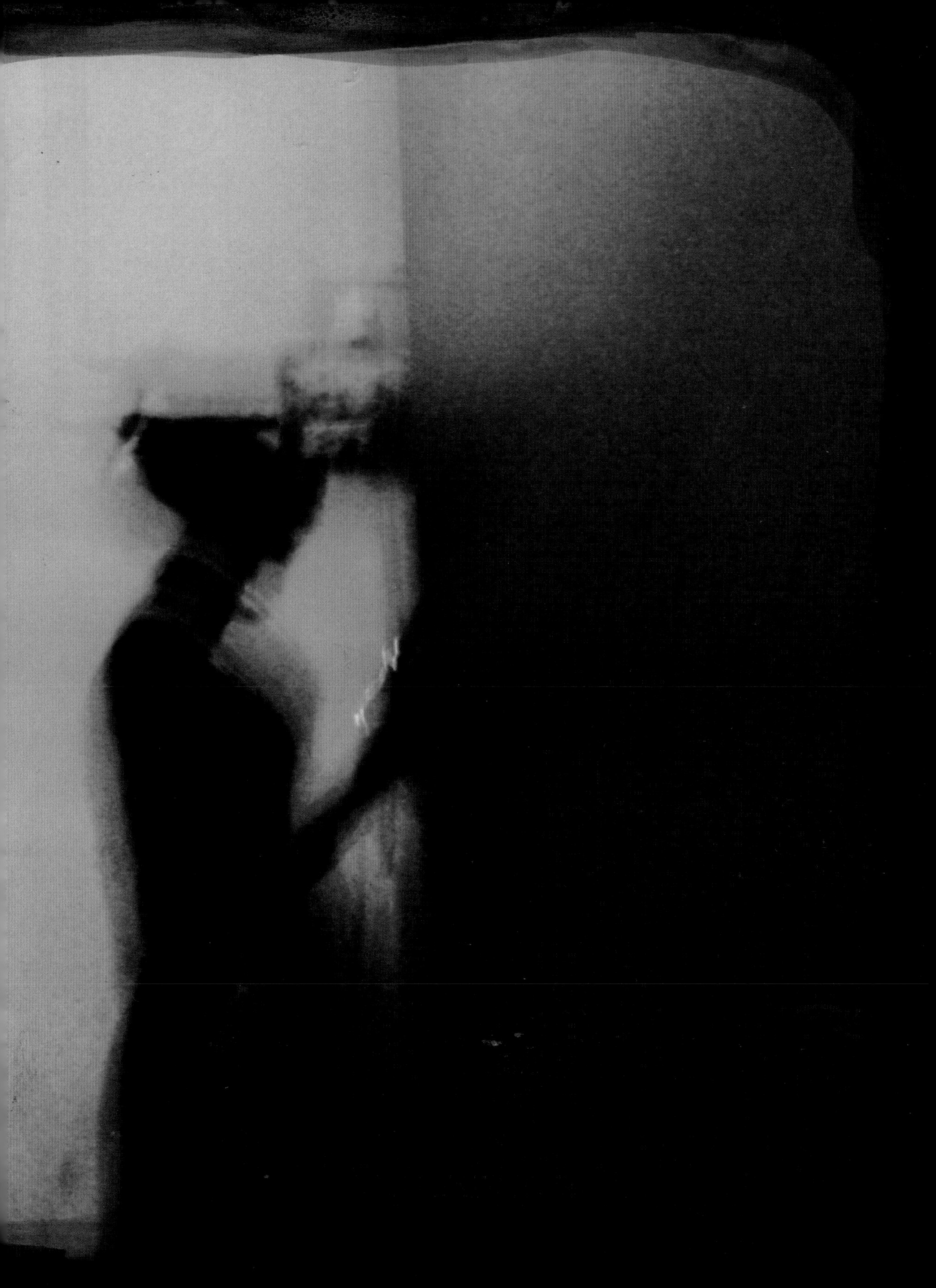

THE STORY OF MI-SU

These are the words of a sex worker in Mae Sot, who was interviewed using questions provided by a sex worker from Vancouver. Many of the images are based on photos by Mi-Su.

MAE SOT, THAILAND.
TODAY. A ROOM. WITH ONLY THE TELEVISION FOR COMPANY.
WAITING FOR THE CLIENT TO COME.

AND MY STORY. THE JOURNEY. HOW I CAME HERE,
STUCK IN MY HEAD.

IT WAS AFTER I TRIED TO SET OUT ON MY OWN.

AFTER MY CHILDHOOD WHEN I PLAYED ALONE, PEACEFULLY.

AFTER MY FATHER BOUGHT ME BACK.

AFTER THE NOODLE HOUSE IN MYAWADDY CLOSED.

AFTER MY MOTHER SOLD ME.

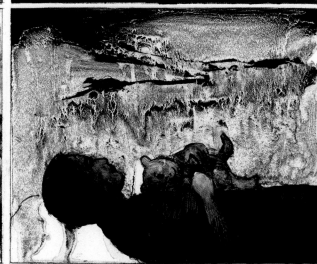

I WAS BORN IN RANGOON.

CHAINED MONKEYS.

THE SMELL OF JASMINE.

SAFFRON, GREEN, GOLD.

WET STREETS.

THE RICKSHAWS.

JUST A BIG CITY.

BUT WE WERE A FAMILY THERE.

MY PARENTS OWNED A NOODLE HOUSE. SOUP, TEA, CAKES.

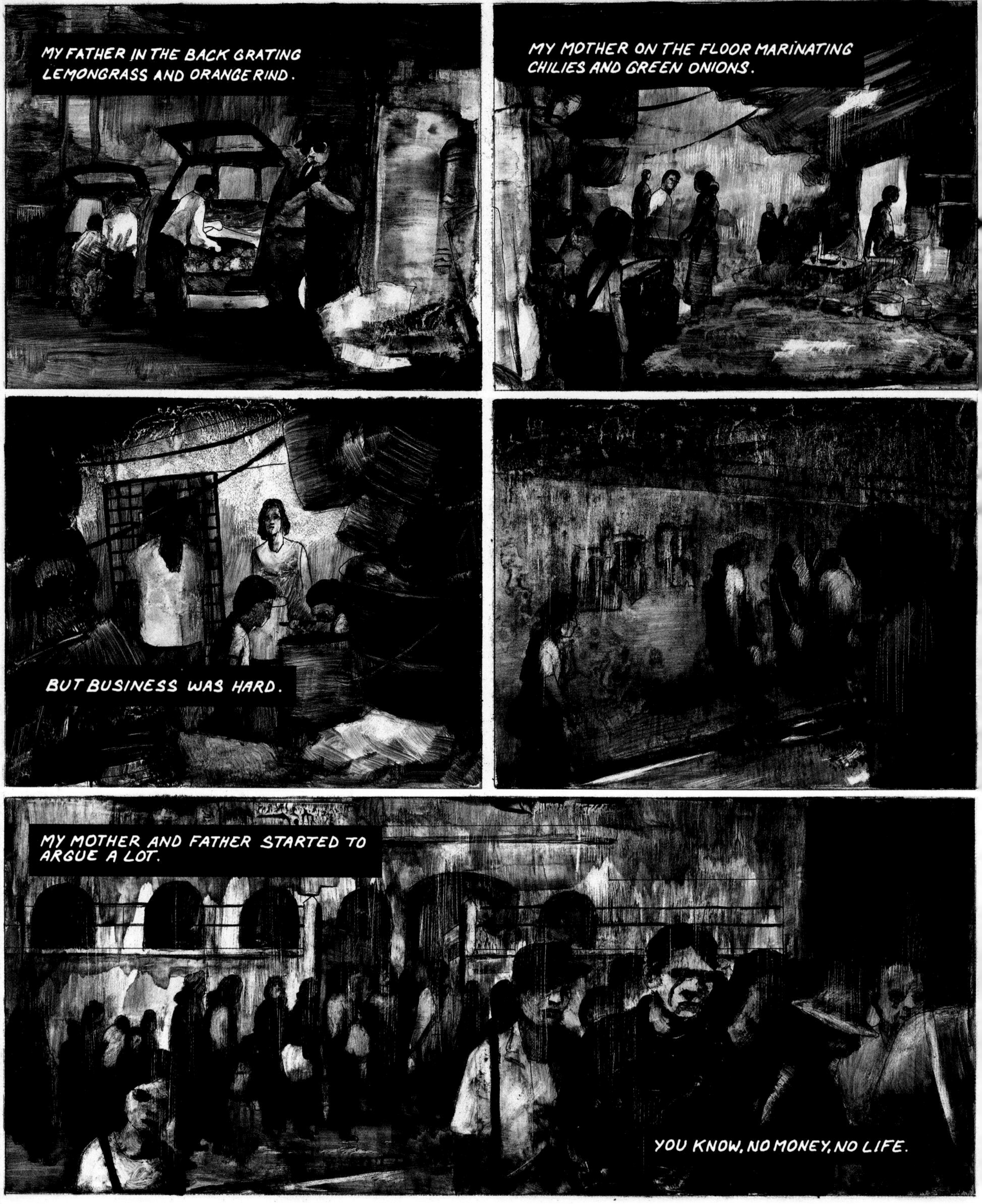
MY FATHER IN THE BACK GRATING LEMONGRASS AND ORANGE RIND.
MY MOTHER ON THE FLOOR MARINATING CHILIES AND GREEN ONIONS.
BUT BUSINESS WAS HARD.
MY MOTHER AND FATHER STARTED TO ARGUE A LOT.
YOU KNOW, NO MONEY, NO LIFE.

THEY GOT A DIVORCE.

I WAS SIX YEARS OLD WHEN I CAME TO MYAWADDY ARMY CAMP.

MY MOTHER WENT TO WORK IN THE PADDY RIGHT AWAY.

SHE LEFT ME WITH A MAN AND HIS WIFE.

SHE SAID, "I WILL COME BACK."

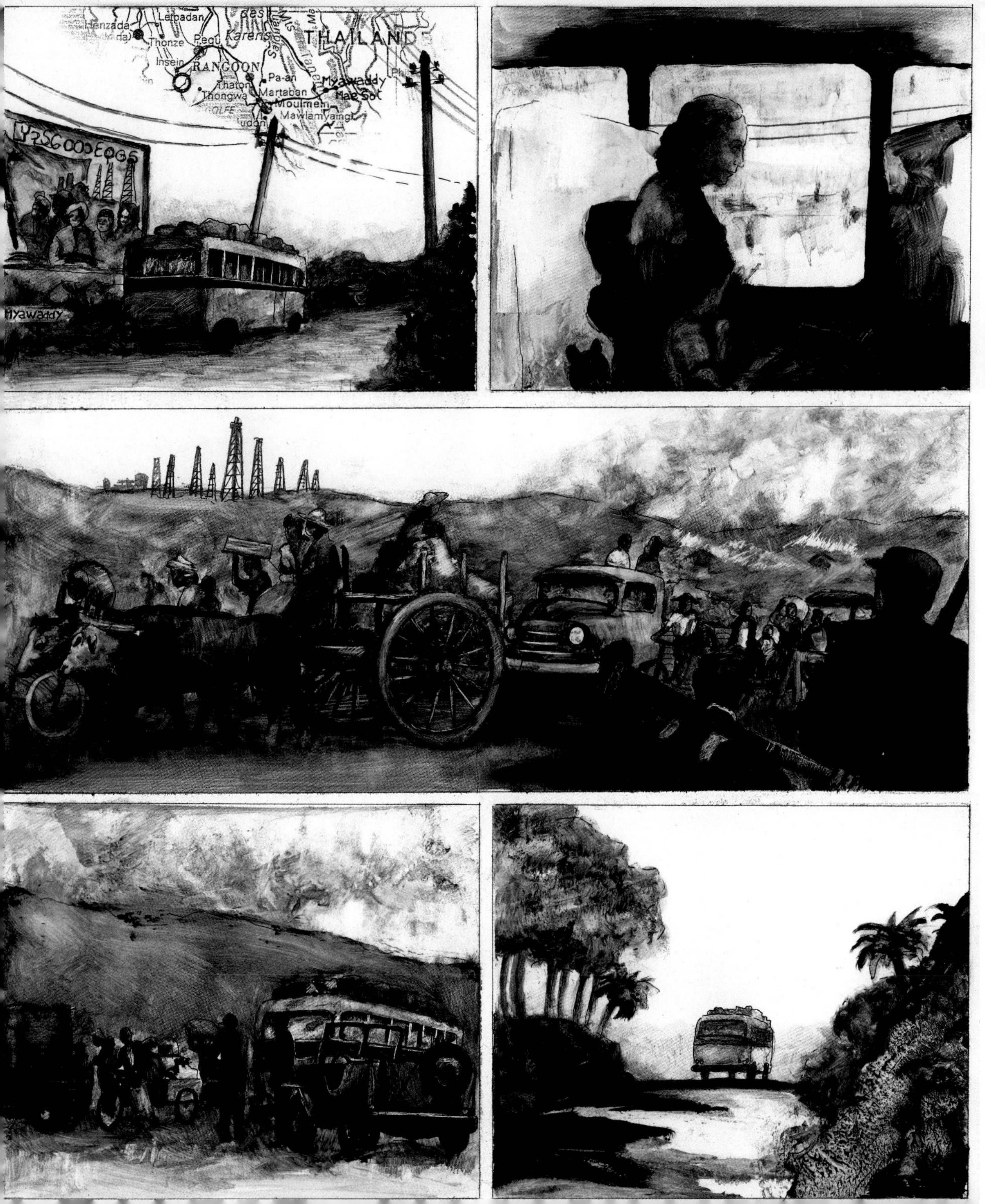

Letpadan
Thonze
Pegu
Karens
THAILANDE
Insein
RANGOON
Pa-an
Thaton
Martaban
Myawaddy
Mae Sot
Thongwa
Moulmein
Mawlamyaing
Myawaddy

THE MAN SAID, "IF YOU GO LOOKING FOR YOUR MOTHER WE WILL FIND YOU AND TIE YOU UP WITH ROPE."

I FOUND OUT THEN THAT MY MOTHER HAD SOLD ME TO THIS MAN AND HIS WIFE.

SOMETIMES THE WIFE WOULD HIT ME ON THE SIDE OF MY HEAD.

BUT LIFE WAS NOT SO BAD.

I HAD RICE AND GOOD CURRY ONCE A DAY.

THEY HAD A FEW ROOMS NEAR THE WATCHTOWER IN MAE TOUNG, WHERE THEY WORKED AT THE MARKET.

ALL DAY I WATCHED THE BABY AND WASHED CLOTHES.

I WAS IN THE STREET WITH THAT BABY WHEN I SAW MY FATHER.

HE SAID, "THAT LOOKS LIKE LITTLE SISTER!". MY BROTHERS WERE WITH HIM, AND I CALLED OUT TO THEM, AND THEY CAME NEAR ENOUGH TO TOUCH.

MY FATHER SAID: "YOU'RE THE DAUGHTER I LOST."

I REMEMBER HOW WE WALKED TOGETHER TO THE ROOMS NEAR THE WATCHTOWER. MY FATHER SAID, "GIVE ME BACK MY CHILD. IF YOU DON'T I'LL TELL THE POLICE".

"WE CAN'T GIVE HER TO YOU," THE MAN SAID. "WE BOUGHT HER." MY FATHER HAD TO PAY THAT MAN EVERYTHING TO GET ME BACK. IT WAS OVER 20.000 BAHT.

I WAS FREE.

MY FATHER SENT ME TO MY ELDEST SISTER WHO HAD A GOOD JOB AT THE BANK.

SHE SAID, "YOU DON'T NEED TO WORK. LET ME TAKE CARE OF YOU."

I KNEW IT WOULDN'T LAST.

ONE DAY I WOULD HAVE TO WALK MY OWN WAY.

I WAS ELEVEN YEARS OLD.

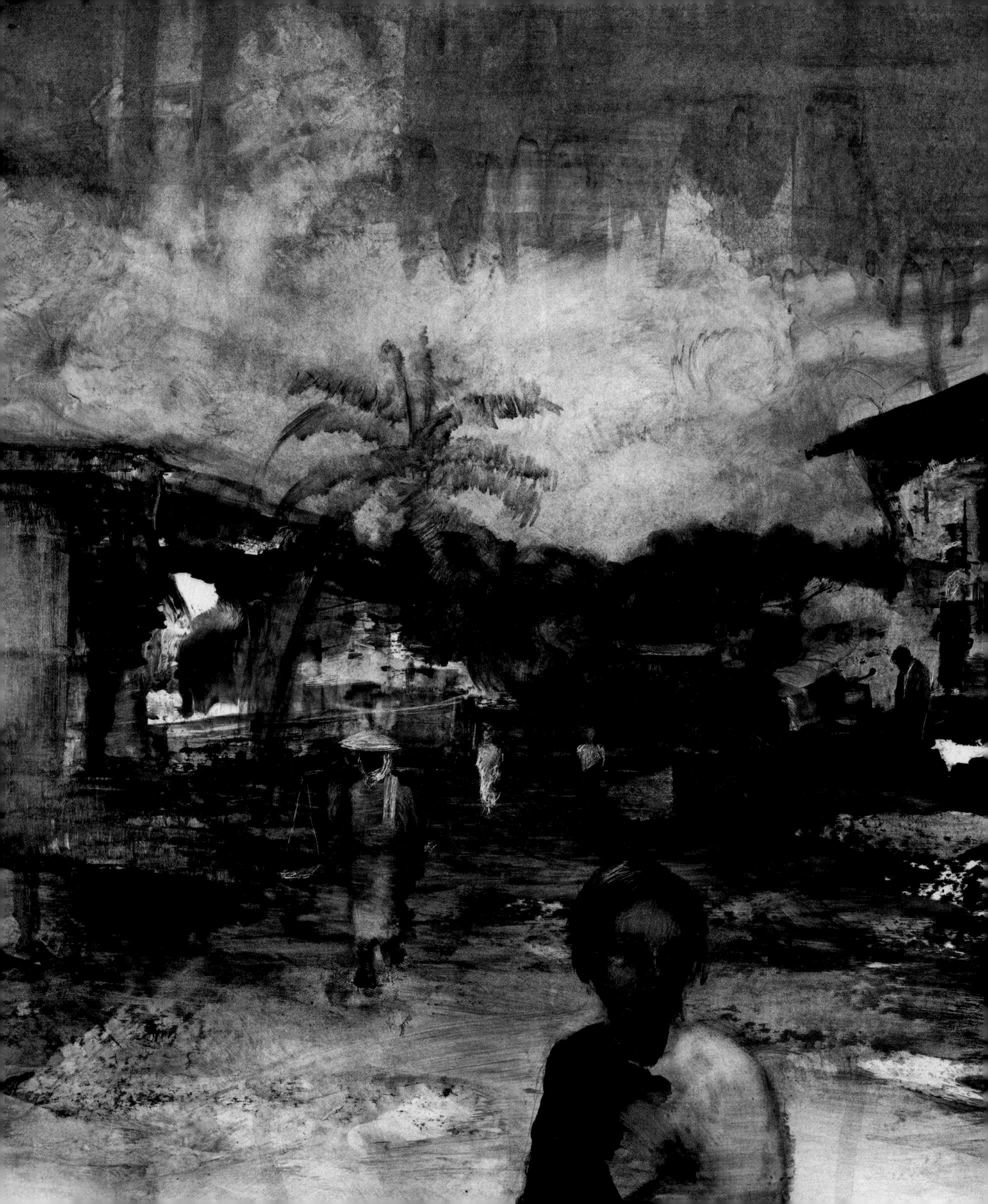

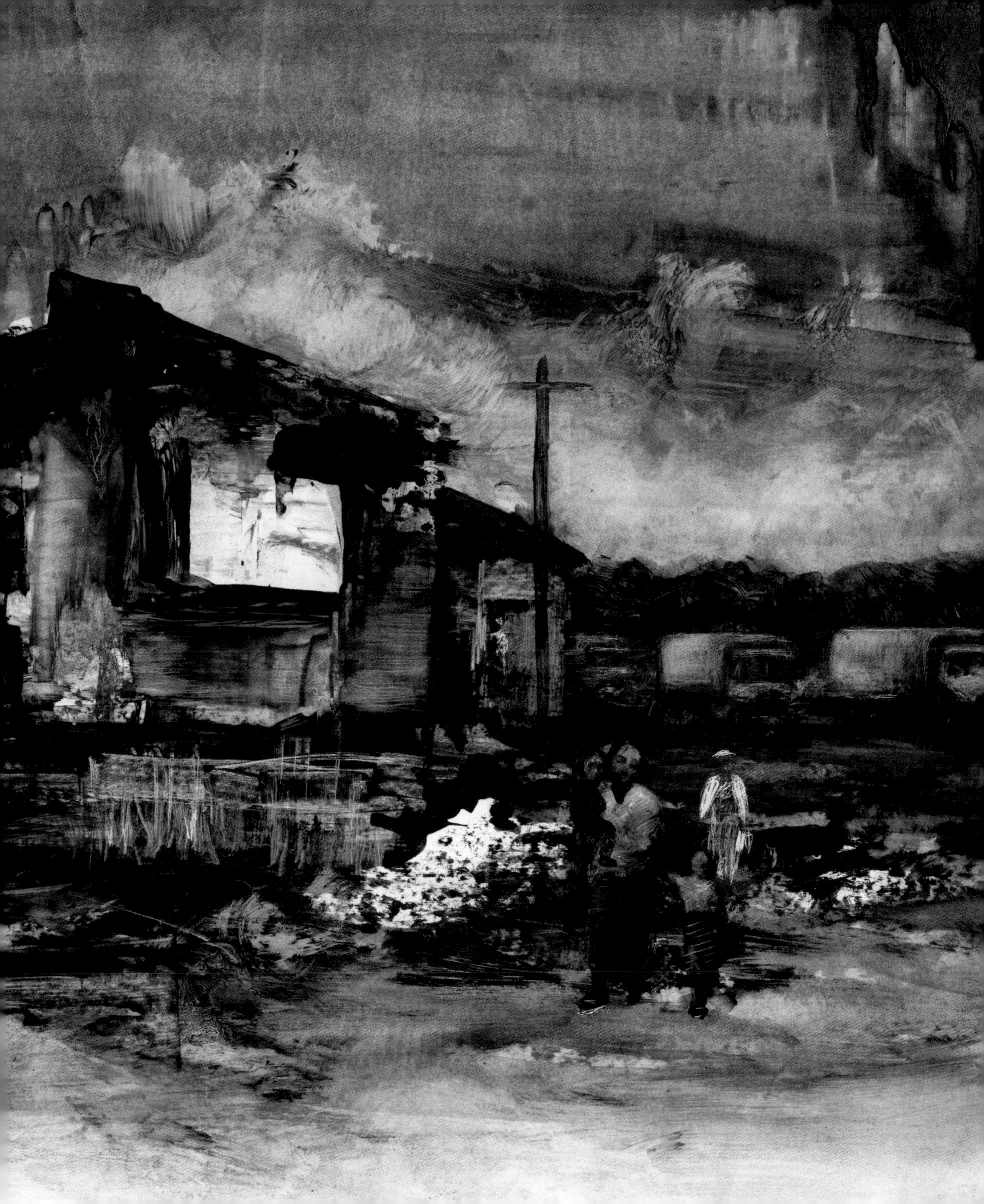

I WENT TO STAY WITH MY SISTER'S FRIEND NAMED AYE AYE.

AND THIS IS WHERE IT BEGAN.

MY VIRGINTY WAS WORTH A LOT.

I GOT ABOUT 6,000 BAHT, AND THE MAMASAN TOOK 1,000.

THEN I WENT BACK TO MYAWADDY, BUT THERE WAS NO WORK THERE.

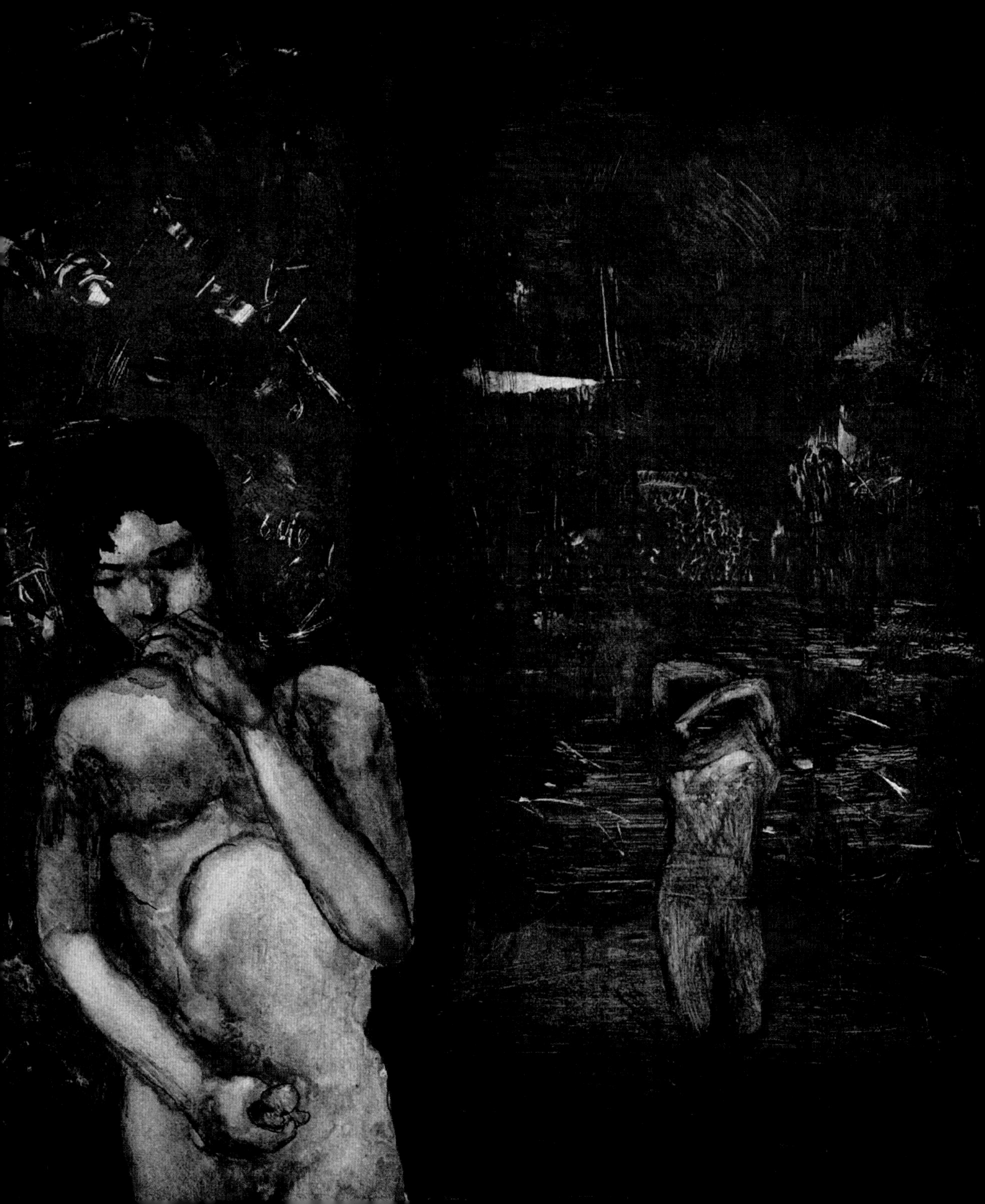

WHEN I AM WITH A MAN HE CAN KISS MY CHEEK, OR HOLD MY BREAST.

AFTERWARD, WE DON'T HUG OR KISS.

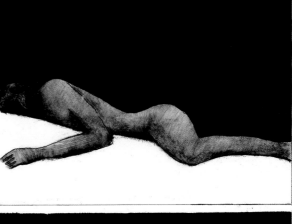

I'M HAPPY WHEN THE CLIENT IS HAPPY.

BUT I WORRY.

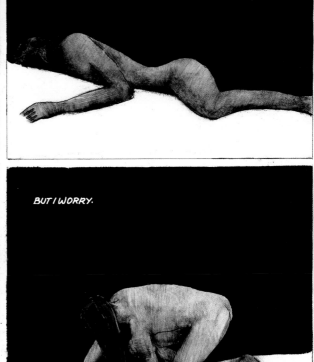

MOST OF ALL, I DISLIKE MY LOWER PARTS.

I WORRY ABOUT HIV, EVEN THOUGH I WASH AND TAKE A TONIC.

I DON'T MAKE SO MUCH MONEY NOW. WHEN I FIRST STARTED THIS JOB I COULD MAKE MONEY TO SEND HOME TO MY FAMILY.

NOW THERE'S NOT MUCH.

I WONDER, WHY DO THEY MAKE A PERSON CHEAPER, LIKE WITH OLD CLOTHES?

I SHOULD GO TO THE HOSPITAL FOR MY BREATHING.

I HAVE A MEMORY OF MY MOTHER THAT I CAN'T FORGET.

I'M YOUNG AND WE'RE SWIMMING AT LAKE LAY.

I CAN'T SWIM AND MY MOTHER

DIVES IN TO SAVE ME.

AND WE ARE BOTH DROWNING.

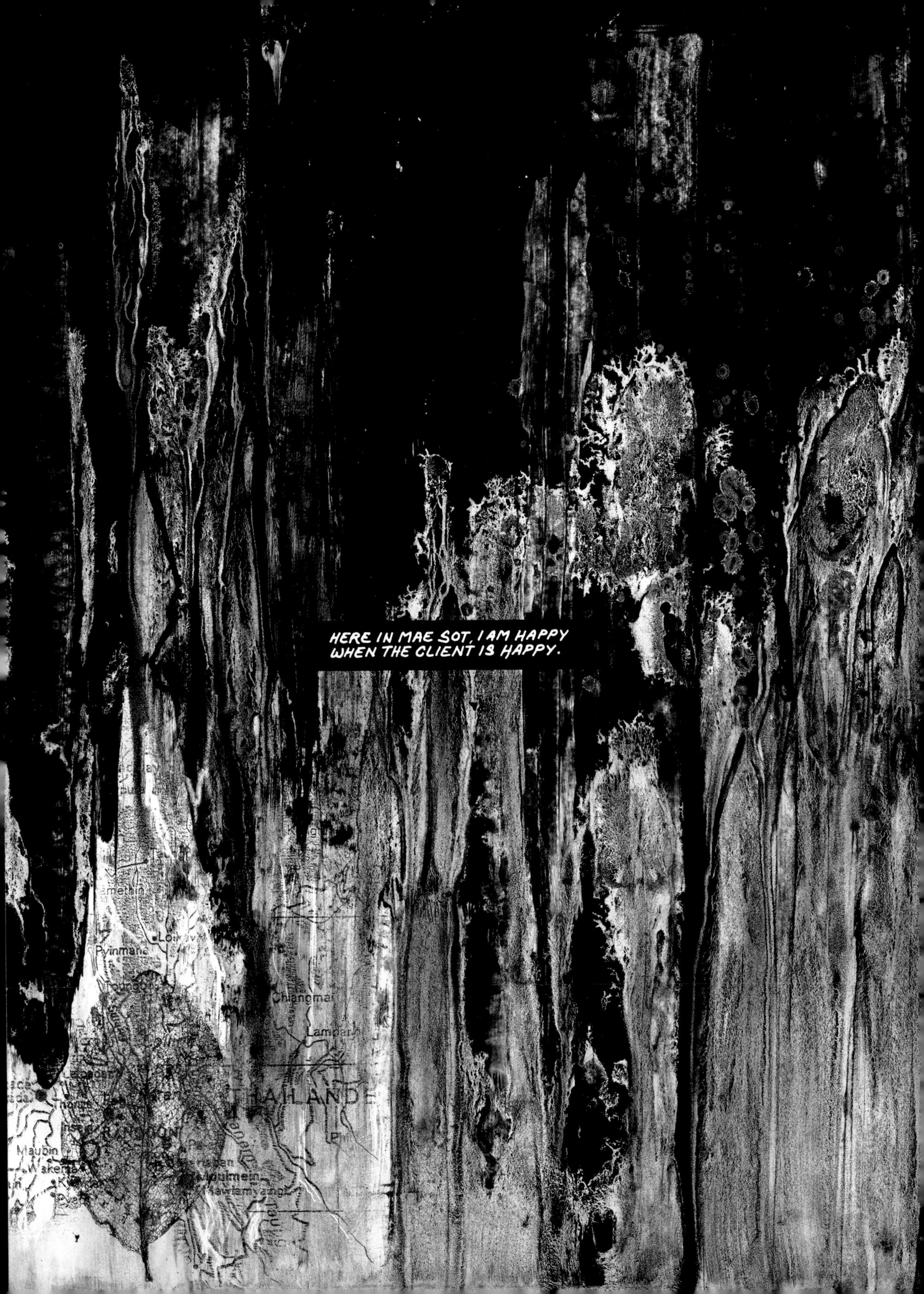
HERE IN MAE SOT, I AM HAPPY WHEN THE CLIENT IS HAPPY.
Chiangmai
Maubin

HELLO, My Name is Stupid.

Mother once told me that if you have bleach on your hands, don't touch yourself down there or it might burst into flames. I have always wanted to see if that were true. That if the Lady made me put the Superman cape on the dog one more time, I would touch myself and shoot flames from down there. And her hair would catch on fire. And maybe she would die.

A story of domestic work. The photos were taken by a 13-year-old Karen girl whose 16-year-old sister works in Bangkok.

SUPER DOG... WILL PROTECT YOU.

Mother always said that I had an imagination like a lovesick hyena. Maybe. I prefer a lovesick tiny monkey.

Even though my breasts still look like sleeping mats and my hands can fit under the cracks of doors, when the Lady is gone, I like to pretend that her house is mine. While she drives away in the white car to buy fish and love songs, I go into her closet and put on her long dresses. I like the black one with the orange buttons that look like smiley faces. I turn the music on. I like her ugly son's music. Mostly the Grateful Dead.

I pretend that the dog is me, and I am the Lady. Go! Go you shit-head and polish my floors. Now! But the dog just stares at me and licks the banister. He's not that much fun at this game. If I did what the dog does, she would send me back.

My home, a place where bananas and mangoes fall from trees. Where the rain makes my hands shine and sounds like angry men running on our roof. I had a secret there. A castle. I would lie in the corner of my white rice bed and watch stars fall from the hole in the roof.

My brothers call me Stupid. I like my name because it makes people smile when I introduce myself.

Mother told me I was born deaf and dumb. I think she said this because I used to let the monkeys out of their bamboo cages at night and follow them up into the tops of trees. Maybe she called me deaf because I would pretend not to hear her as she ran after me with her bamboo stick.

The monkeys were my heart. My I=love=you=friends.

Maybe the dog here will become an okay friend. Yesterday as I was trying the Lady's black wig, he barked when she came home. I had time to put the wig back in the silver box and run to the bathroom. Just in time, because she walked by me smelling like old flower-water. She likes me to clean the floor with a yellow toothbrush so that it will shine and reflect her feet. Even though they are ugly.

The really Ugly Mister and the Lady say that I am lucky to be here. That I could have ended up a dead Karen in the jungle or eaten by the AIDS in the refugee camps. At night when they finish their food, they give me their plates and I take them back to my room. I lick the plates clean. Maybe that's why the dog likes me. We both like to lick plates. I think he thinks I am a dog too. I don't want to hurt his feelings and tell him the truth.

I lost my mother in the jungle. After the angry men burned our rice fields, Mother ran with me and my brother. Her hand was wet and salty and she ran too fast. And then she was gone.

I don't miss her though. She was a bitch.

At night in the jungle, I would pretend to be a cuckoo bird looking for my castle in my monkey kingdom. I would lie in my rice bed and listen to the pink music. I would fall asleep in the monkey's warm hands. When the rains started, I took a knife and cut my hair off. I covered myself with mud and hoped I would start to grow roots, just like the wild lilies.

Someone saw me on a road and took me to a city where men brush their eyebrows with tiny brushes and there are cars everywhere. It's loud.

Stupid's list of things to do from the Lady: Wash underthings and hang to dry in your room. Water the bonsai and give it sunlight bath. Wash and wipe flat surfaces. NO DUST!!! Don't touch anything. Wash all the clothes in the closets if they have been there for more than a week. Iron. Put oranges, cookies, rice, and flowers in front of the Buddha. Bow and say thank you. Wash dog each day. Brush his teeth with toothpaste. On special days, put on the Superman cape. Sit quietly in your room when you are finished and don't move until the Lady says yes, go.

At night when I don't move in my room, I tell myself again and again that I am a statue. Maybe that's why the dog and I might become okay friends. He comes to see me and licks my face and curls up beside my running-away heart.

We arrive at a house behind white iron gates. Inside, two Burmese men sit in a sparsely furnished room. The floor is speckled with brown tile, afternoon sun making patterns on the floor. Star patterns. I notice, because I don't want to look the men in the eyes.

I can tell that even Saw-Po is nervous.

One of the men takes us up creaky stairs and opens a door into a small room. He closes the door and we can hear him walk away. In front of us, five girls eat crackers and watch a Robbie Williams video. Several appear to be under 15. I watch the blue screen with them, equally transfixed as Robbie Williams, stealthlike, slides over a piano in his vintage tuxedo.

The room smells sour; I guess
they're not allowed to open the
windows. There are no beds, only
plastic mats with faded flowered
bedding. A girl climbs out of the closet
and into the room. She was hiding from
a potential customer, she says.

She wears a white pressed blouse
and a blue skirt - it looks almost like a
uniform. She is thin, so thin. Shiny hair,
melted caramel skin. Her hands knot and
twist invisible braids and she bows her
head, her hair covering her face.

It's very quiet in here.

She writes this down for me in Burmese:
"I am 16. I want to learn English and be a
teacher."

It doesn't matter that we don't say a lot
to each other. Something lovely happens.
She is looking right at me, and I at her.
There is a comfort that comes from feeling
less alone in this world.

One night, while I was lying on my bed looking to the
moon and stars that shone over my house, I felt sad
and lonely. I remembered my village, my home, and my
dog. His name is Pah Kaw. What will happen to him?

My dog is very beautiful. One day, I had to go to my
farm, far away through the jungle. I felt afraid
to travel alone, I had no friend to go with me. I
looked at Pah Kaw and asked, "Will you go with me?"
He looked at me like he was smiling, wagged his tail
and came. Sometimes he followed me, sometimes he
went before me, sometimes at my right, sometimes at
my left. He guarded me until we reached the farm. He
understands my words, and sometimes he talks to me.
I only hear the voice. I don't understand the words.

I love my dog so much. I can't say more about him than
that, because I didn't understand his words at all.

Pah Kaw was not at home when I left my village.
He had gone into the jungle, hunting. When he came
back, he would have been lonely and sad. He would
have searched for me. Dear Pah Kaw, are you facing
difficulties because of me? You would suffer more
than me. You would think your owner didn't love you,
and forsook you. You would say, where is my master
who loved me? Where is my home? What is the meaning of
home for me?

He would have found someone to stay with. He would
never die for feeling hungry.

Oh! Pah Kaw, I loved you, but I had to forsake you.
Please forgive me.

Myawaddy, Burma